THIRTEEN WAYS of LOOKING at a BLACK BOY

Tony Medina & 13 Artists

Penny Candy BOOKS

Penny Candy Books
Oklahoma City & Savannah
Text © 2018 Tony Medina
Illustrations © 2018 individual artists

SUSTAINABLE FORESTRY INITIATIVE
Certified Chain of Custody
Promoting Sustainable Forestry
www.sfiprogram.org
SFI-01268
SFI label applies to the text stock

The Sustainable Forestry Initiative® program integrates the perpetual growing and harvesting of trees with the protection of wildlife, plants, soils and water.

Acknowledgments: The poems in *Thirteen Ways of Looking at a Black Boy* were first published in slightly different form under the title "Anacostia Suite (13 Ways of Looking at a Black Boy)," in *Revise the Psalm: Work Celebrating the Writing of Gwendolyn Brooks*, edited by Quraysh Ali Lansana & Sandra Jackson-Opoku (Curbside Splendor, 2017), and subsequently in the *Rumpus*.
Illustrations & photos: See additional acknowledgments on pages 33–38.
Design: Shanna Compton, shannacompton.com

22 21 20 19 18   1 2 3 4 5
ISBN-13: 978-0-9987999-4-0 (hardcover)

Books for the kid in *all* of us
www.pennycandybooks.com

DEDICATION

For Black and Brown children
    Whose every breath is affirmation
Against erasure
    Whose very being is confirmation
For generations

Thirteen Ways: An Introduction

Black boys scrape their knees—they bleed
Black boys cry and scream—they tackle life like air
Gliding on wind—basking in a breeze

Black boys sit beneath trees—inhale fresh-cut grass
And dream
Black boys play with building blocks, are fascinated
By clocks—cradle skateboards under their arms

Black boys love basketball and books—toss footballs
And leaf through pages lost in stories and myths
Black boys love comic books and superheroes—
Are heroes to little sisters and brothers

Black boys love popcorn and watching movies
Love their grandmas and grandpas
Black boys hug and kiss their moms
And emulate their dads
Black boys wear their daddy's shoes and ties
Smear shaving cream on their smooth faces
Giggling in steamy mirrors

Black boys shine bright in sunlight
Build snowmen and have snowball fights
Black boys study the stars—looking
Through telescopes, lie on their backs
In tall grass, staring at the blanket of blue sky
At all the eyes smiling and twinkling
Down on them

Black boys like to hum and drum
Bebop hip hop—like to dance and sing
Jazz and scream

Black boys are three dimensions of beauty
Black boys go to church
Ride buses, go to school
Sit on stoops, fly kites, shoot hoops

Black boys like to sit in their quiet
And think about things

Black boys are made of flesh—
Not clay

Black boys have bones and blood
And feelings

Black boys have minds that thrive with ideas
Like bees around a hive
Black boys are alive with wonder and possibility
With hopes and dreams

Black boys be bouquets of tanka
Bunched up like flowers
They be paint blotched into a myriad of colors
Across the canvases of our hearts

We celebrate their preciousness and creativity
We cherish their lives

—TONY MEDINA

Anacostia Angel

Fly bow tie like wings
  Brown eyes of a brown angel
His kool-aid smile sings
  Mama's little butterfly
Daddy's dimple grin so wide

Floyd Cooper

Little Mister May

My granny made me this suit
   So I could look nice for God
She's always at church
   Her Bible's older than me
It's heavier than can be

Cozbi A. Cabrera

Images of Kin

South East Benin mask
   Face like a road map of kin
Brought back from the past
   Resurrected dignity
Flesh of onyx majesty

Skip Hill

The Charmer

Between you and me
   All of the girls like my smile
The boys be jealous
   Call me bubblehead and laugh
The girls roll their eyes and sass

Tiffany McKnight

Robert Liu-Trujillo

One-Way Ticket

Payday don't pay much
  Every breath I take is taxed
The kind of life where
  I'll have to take out a loan
To pay back them other loans

Lazy Hazy Daze

Summertime on stoop
  Forehead sweat like ice cream tears
Hiding from the sun
  Wishing for the rain to come
Cool us like johnny pump spray

My Soul to Keep

We preachers' brothers
   Grew up crawlin' under pews
Splintered as Christ's cross
   While Daddy spit the Gospel
From sanctified side-eye lips

Shawn K. Alexander

Kesha Bruce

Do Not Enter

Ashes pepper sky
  Over deserted landscape
Of broke-down buildings
  And cars propped on cinderblocks
Where hope hurtled through the wind

Brianna McCarthy

Street Corner Prophet

Dreadlock halo crown
   Jesus show up everywhere
In a black parka
   Here in Anacostia
Winter corner's sacred sons

Athlete's Broke Bus Blues

Know how many times
  I done missed this broke-down bus
Hardly catch my breath
  Running as fast as can be,
Wave at this bus leaving me

R. Gregory Christie

Brothers Gonna Work It Out

We righteous Black men
    Patrol the soul of this 'hood
Raise young bloods proper
    To be the kings that they are
Crowned glory of our future

Ekua Holmes

Cat at the Curb

Sandwiched between curb
 And black radial tire
A cat with nine lives
 Not yet spent contemplates life
Springtime days bunched up like grass

Javaka Steptoe

Chandra Cox

Givin' Back to the Community

I went to this school
    When I was a shawty rock
Breakin' in the yard
    Wanted to be a rap star—
But a teacher's not too far!

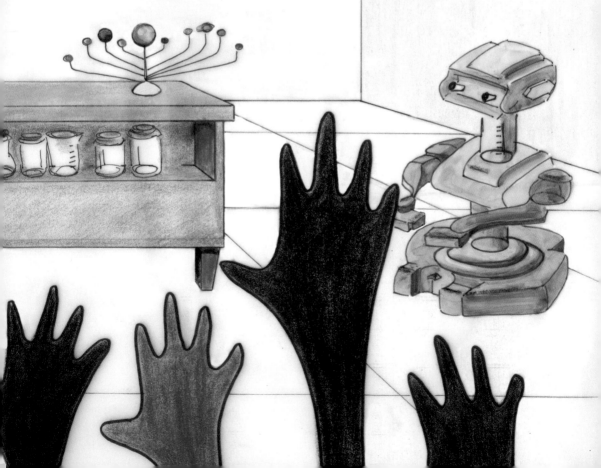

About the Poet

TONY MEDINA, two-time winner of the Paterson Prize for Books for Young People (*DeShawn Days* and *I and I, Bob Marley*), is the author/editor of nineteen books for adults and young readers. A Professor of Creative Writing at Howard University, Medina has received the Langston Hughes Society Award, the first African Voices Literary Award, and has been nominated for Pushcart Prizes for his poems. Jacar Press recently published his anthology *Resisting Arrest: Poems to Stretch the Sky*, on police violence and brutalities perpetrated on people of color. Tu Books published Medina's debut graphic novel *I Am Alfonso Jones* in 2017. For more, see tonymedina.org. • *Tony's photo © Aldon Lynn Nielsen.*

About the Artists

ANACOSTIA ANGEL • With over one hundred children's books to his name, **FLOYD COOPER** is a master craftsman of children's literature and illustration. He has received numerous awards and praise for his work, including three Coretta Scott King Honors, an NAACP Image Award, the Jane Addams Peace Honor, the Simon Wiesenthal Gold Medal, and the prestigious Sankae Award of Japan. He is the 2018 artist for the U.S. Postal Service KWANZAA Forever stamp. This Tulsa native now makes his home in Easton, PA, with his wife Velma, sons Dayton and Kai, daughter-in-law Melissa, and grandson Niko. • *Illustration © Floyd Cooper. Floyd's photo © Jacob Blickenstaff.*

LITTLE MISTER MAY • **COZBI A. CABRERA** is the award-winning illustrator of many picture books, including *Thanks a Million* by acclaimed poet Nikki Grimes. She is the author/illustrator of the forthcoming picture book, *My Hair Is a Garden* (Albert Whitman, 2018), as well as the illustrator for the bilingual picture book *Luca's Bridge/El Puente de Luca* by Mariana Llanos (Penny Candy Books, 2018), and *Exquisite: The Poetry and Life of Gwendolyn Brooks* by Suzanne Slade (Abrams, 2019). Cozbi's handmade collectible cloth dolls (muñecas), which she makes in honor of her Honduran heritage, have been featured on the *Oprah Winfrey Show* and in *Martha Stewart Living*. • *Illustration © Cozbi A. Cabrera. Cozbi's photo © Amilcar Cabrera.*

IMAGES OF KIN • SKIP HILL is a mixed-media visual artist and illustrator of the picture book *A Gift from Greensboro* (Penny Candy Books, 2016) by poet Quraysh Ali Lansana. His illustrations for *A Gift from Greensboro* have been described by book critics as "brimming with life," "nostalgia with a psychedelic twist," and "a salve to the eye and soul." Skip's body of work is comprised of large scale murals, drawings, and collage paintings that weave a rich tapestry of aesthetic styles sourced from folk art, African masks, comic books, Japanese Ukiyo-e prints, street art, and art history. Skip's contribution to *Thirteen Ways of Looking at a Black Boy* is inspired by his fascination with West African Ife bronze sculpture, by Hip-Hop culture, and by his own black boy, his son Adam. Skip Hill's art is in private and public collections throughout the US, Europe, and Latin America. • *Illustration & artist photo © Skip Hill.*

THE CHARMER • Tulsa native and current Oklahoma City resident TIFFANY McKNIGHT received her BFA in Studio Art with a focus in Printmaking from the University of Oklahoma in 2012. She is the author of *NUVEAU: The Future of Patterns* (Penelope Editions, 2017), an intricate coloring book for pattern lovers. Her patterns can be found on labels of San Francisco's Clearly Kombucha products, on luxury wallpaper produced in collaboration with SixTwelve OKC and Ketch Design Centre, and on wrapping paper for the *Curbside Chronicle*'s Wrap Up Homelessness program. In 2017 Tiffany was chosen as one of the contributing artists to Factory Obscura, an art collective bringing a new and interactive experience to Oklahoma City. • *Illustration © Tiffany McKnight. Tiffany's photo © Romy Owens.*

ONE-WAY TICKET • ROBERT LIU-TRUJILLO is the author and illustrator of *Furqan's First Flat Top* (Come Bien Books, 2016), as well as several bilingual picture books. He loves social

justice, storytelling, mural making, and ice cream. He's a cofounder of the Trust Your Struggle Collective, a contributor to *Rad Dad*, and the founder of Come Bien Books. He lives in Oakland, CA with his wife and son. • *Illustration © Robert Liu-Trujillo. Robert's photo © Scott La Rockwell.*

LAZY HAZY DAZE • **KEITH MALLETT** is an artist who lives with his wife in San Diego. His website is keithmallett.com. • *Illustration © Keith Mallett. Keith's photo © Dianne Mallett.*

MY SOUL TO KEEP • SHAWN K. ALEXANDER is a graduate of the Cooper Union School of Art (BFA) and the University of Michigan (MFA), and has worked on film and television sets. His digital art can be found on Instagram under the handle @popcorn.on.mute. Many thanks to Tony Medina for the opportunity to illustrate one of his tanka poems. • *Illustration & artist photo © Shawn K. Alexander.*

DO NOT ENTER • KESHA BRUCE creates richly textured and visually complex artworks that explore the connections between memory, personal mythology, and magical-spiritual belief. Born and raised in Iowa, she completed a BFA from the University of Iowa before earning an MFA in painting from Hunter College in New York City. Kesha has been awarded fellowships from the New York Foundation for the Arts (NYFA), the Vermont Studio Center, the CAMAC Foundation, and received a Puffin Foundation Grant for her work with Artist's Books. Her work is included in the permanent collections of the Smithsonian Museum of African American History and Culture, the Amistad Center for Art and Culture, the University of Iowa Women's Center, the En Foco Photography Collection, and the Museum of Modern Art/Franklin Furnace Artist Book Collection. • *Illustration & artist photo © Kesha Bruce.*

STREET CORNER PROPHET • BRIANNA MCCARTHY is a mixed-media visual communicator working and living in Trinidad + Tobago. She is a self-taught artist and aims to create a new discourse examining issues of beauty, stereotypes, and representation, as well as the documentation of the process—particularly poignant in an ever smaller digitally connected world. Her form takes shape through masking and performance art, fabric collage, traditional media, and installation pieces. • *Illustration © Brianna McCarthy. Brianna's photo © Arnaldo James.*

ATHLETE'S BROKE BUS BLUES • R. GREGORY CHRISTIE is a five-time recipient of the Coretta Scott King Honor Award in Illustration. He is the designer of the 2013 Kwanzaa Forever stamp for the United States Post Office, a two-time recipient of the *New York Times* Ten Best Illustrated Children's Books of the Year Award, and an NAACP Image Award recipient. His most recent book, *Freedom in Congo Square*, won a 2017 Caldecott honor. He has illustrated more than fifty books, a multitude of magazine images, and many jazz album covers. You can visit him at his Decatur, GA, bookstore, GAS-ART GIFTS, or online at www.gas-art.com. • *Illustration & artist photo © R. Gregory Christie.*

BROTHERS GONNA WORK IT OUT • EKUA HOLMES's collages celebrate the vibrancy of urban life and the joys and challenges of childhood. She was the recipient of a 2013 Brother Thomas Fellowship from the Boston Foundation for her contributions to the Boston arts community. In 2014 she became the first African-American woman to be appointed to the Boston Arts Commission. Holmes's debut as a picture book illustrator, *Voice of Freedom: Fannie Lou Hamer: The Spirit of the Civil Rights Movement* (Candlewick, 2015) by Carole Boston Weatherford, received a Silver Medal from the Society of Illustrator's Original Art exhibition, the Robert F. Sibert and Randolph Caldecott

Honors, and a Coretta Scott King John Steptoe New Illustrator Award. • *Illustration ©
Ekua Holmes. Ekua's photo © Clennon L. King, Augustine Monica Films.*

CAT AT THE CURB • **JAVAKA STEPTOE**'s debut picture book, *In Daddy's Arms I Am Tall:
African Americans Celebrating Fathers* (Lee & Low Books, 1998), earned him a Coretta
Scott King Illustrator Award and a nomination for Outstanding Children's Literature Work
at the NAACP Image Awards. Since then Steptoe has illustrated and/or written more
than a dozen books for young readers, collaborating with some of the top names in the
business, such as Walter Dean Myers, Nikki Grimes, and Karen English. His latest book,
Radiant Child: The Story of Young Artist Jean-Michel Basquiat (Little, Brown, 2016) won
the 2017 Caldecott Medal and 2017 Coretta Scott King Illustrator Award. • *Illustration ©
Javaka Steptoe. Javaka's photo © Hidden Chapel Studios.*

GIVIN' BACK TO THE COMMUNITY • **CHANDRA COX**, Professor and Head of the Department
of Art + Design, College of Design, North Carolina State University, is a practicing artist
and designer who explores a wide palette of mediums, from paper collage, to acrylic
paint, to three-dimensional forms. Cox's work has been displayed in numerous museums
and galleries around the country, including the North Carolina Museum of Art (Raleigh,
NC) and the Museum of Science and Industry (Chicago, IL). She has also illustrated a
children's book, *Christmas Makes Me Think* (Lee & Low Books, 2001) by Tony Medina.
Cox has received the Outstanding Teacher Award and the Undergraduate Distinguished
Professor Award at NC State University. • *Illustration © Chandra Cox. Chandra's photo
© Meghan Palmer.*

Notes

ON THE TITLE: *Thirteen Ways of Looking at a Black Boy* riffs off of two major works of poetry: Wallace Stevens's poem, "Thirteen Ways of Looking at a Blackbird," and Raymond R. Patterson's poetry collection, *Twenty-Six Ways of Looking at a Black Man*, a Black Arts Movement classic responding to Stevens's pastoral meditation. Also of note is Dr. Henry Louis Gates Jr.'s collection of essays, *Thirteen Ways of Looking at a Black Man*. Although I love birds, and I am a man, I chose to focus on the beauty of Black boys who, in certain light, can be considered an endangered species.

ON THE TANKA: The poems in this beautifully illustrated book are written in the tanka form. Tanka is a Japanese syllabic verse form, much like the haiku. But whereas haiku consists of seventeen syllables distributed along three lines, the tanka consists of thirty-one syllables distributed along five lines. It has the first three lines of the haiku: 5-7-5, with an additional 7-7 syllabic breakdown. Tanka are really fun and challenging to write. I try to write mine where every line can stand alone; and I try and focus on making images more than telling or explaining. I like to let the images show the ideas, which makes for more interesting and powerful poetry. You should give it a try!

ON PLACE IN POETRY: In poetry, as in all literature, place always plays an important role. Although many of the tanka can be situated in many different places, for they have a more general, universal appeal, some of the tanka do refer to a place called Anacostia. Anacostia is a Southeast section of Washington, DC, located east of the Anacostia River and named after Nacotchtank Native Americans who settled along the Anacostia River and who were forced northward in 1668 due to war. It is also a historically black neighborhood of Washington, DC, which is quickly becoming more and more gentrified. Anacostia is where freedom fighter Frederick Douglass made his home from 1877 to 1895. The tanka in *Thirteen Ways of Looking at a Black Boy* were originally composed from photographs of residents of Anacostia; thus, the references to Anacostia. Yet I believe they still yield a universal appeal where anyone can relate to the stories in the poems.

THANK YOU

I would like to thank everyone responsible for this beautiful Penny Candy book: my publishers, Alexis Orgera and Chad Reynolds; our designer, Shanna Compton; the great artists whose dynamic work make the magic of children's literature come to life (in order of appearance): Floyd Cooper, Cozbi A. Cabrera, Skip Hill, Tiffany McKnight, Robert Liu-Trujillo, Keith Mallett, Shawn K. Alexander, Kesha Bruce, Brianna McCarthy, R. Gregory Christie, Ekua Holmes, Javaka Steptoe, and Chandra Cox. I also need to thank Quraysh Ali Lansana, for the good word.

—TONY MEDINA

APR 2018